My Life with Foxes

My Life with Foxes

ERIC ASHBY

ROBERT HALE · LONDON

ISBN 0 7090 6561 2

Robert Hale Limited
Clerkenwell House
Clerkenwell Green
London EC1R 0HT

2 4 6 8 10 9 7 5 3

Typeset by
Derek Doyle & Associates, Liverpool.
Colour separations by Tenon & Polert Scanning Ltd.
Printed by Kyodo, Singapore

Contents

To Eileen, without whose encouragement, patience and help,
this book would not have been possible.

Foreword

At daybreak, in that lilac time between the worlds of the dark and light, you can stand in the fields, copses and wastegrounds and, if you're silent, if you're still, you can see one of the most beautiful animals on earth. You can do this anywhere in our land – on every new day of the year. The creature is not rare. It is sleek, soft and charming, but it is a predator and, for all its bravado, it is difficult to get to know. All it takes is a lifetime of curiosity, patience and careful observation. All it takes is years of dedication, effort and endeavour, and the reward for this extraordinary devotion lies in your hands.

Eric Ashby's book is not a scientific treatise, full of figures and graphs, but it is no less precise. His observations bear the mark of a great naturalist – someone who instinctively knows when to stop and listen and half knows what will happen next. It is also a work of passion, his adoration of these creatures pours from the pages; they are his friends with whom he has shared tender moments and tragedies. It is the story of the many lives that have scurried through one life of love.

Few books such as this remain to be written. Truly accomplished naturalists are a severely endangered species. Our modern world is short on the time it takes to hone and honour their skills. In our wham-glam, flash and brash age the calm and gentle lie hidden from view in quiet country gardens and rusty beds of bracken. Theirs is a world of which we can normally only dream but here is a diary which opens a small window into that elusive world. It is a little treasure that will leave a great mark. In its wake you will think of Eric Ashby every time your headlights spill sparkling gold into roadside eyes and the pretty trot and big brush of a fox slips away. That is an enchanting legacy for any man.

Chris Packham, 2000
Naturalist and Broadcaster

Preface

The natural habitat of the country fox has been deteriorating rapidly for many years. A daunting array of hazards now stands between each fox and its survival: huntsmen and women continue to fend off the intense controversy which surrounds their sport; a growing number of trigger-happy newcomers bring suburbia into the countryside, responding thoughtlessly to the wilfully inaccurate, widely accepted

Badger Cottage with fox pens covering a quarter of an acre in the New Forest

portrayal of the fox; and the steady encroachment of new roads and heavy traffic into the country leads to more and more lone cubs and dying foxes being found by the roadside. The wilderness is the fox's only true home; but in the midst of these dangers, life in the wild becomes impossible for a great many foxes.

For fourteen years now, my wife and I have cared for a number of injured or abandoned foxes brought to us at our home in the New Forest. These years have been for us a time not only of devotion but also of reward and of learning. Looking after these foxes has made us aware of their individuality and has allowed us a much deeper understanding of the true nature of this remarkable animal – a nature conspicuously at odds with the populist perception. It is this privileged personal insight which has inspired and informed the following pages.

1 Vicky's Litter

Ever since we first found ourselves caring for foxes, vixens and dog foxes have lived together in our pens, free to share their time and space with each other as they see fit. It is notoriously difficult for foxes to breed in captivity, and any dreams we might have had of their producing cubs always seemed likely to remain dreams. As time passed, however, our understanding of the foxes' needs became more informed and intuitive; the pens became more numerous and the wide grass runs more expansive. The conditions in which our foxes live continually improved, edging closer towards a more natural environment. At the beginning of spring 1990, during the breeding season, Vicky (a vixen who had been with us for four years) and Jacky (a dog fox who had been with us for three years) began to spend considerably more time in each other's company and seemed to have become mates. Scientifically, vixens are supposed to be receptive for three days each year, but she could come into season again should she not be mated during that period. Three days fitted quite well with notes in Eileen's diary:

22 February Vicky growling at the fussy close attentions of Jacky.
23 February Vicky screaming a lot and boxing.
24 February Vicky screaming a lot and excited during evening.
26 February Vicky still a little excited when Jacky came near but she was obviously tired.

The next day the rut was over with Vicky wanting to be left alone to have a well-earned rest.

Jacky and Vicky playfully boxing each other!

At this time of year the days are still short and the long nights bitterly cold and although this is when foxes are active, understandably we cannot monitor this activity. Occasionally we would hear sounds of chasing and play and perhaps a growl or scream, just the same as we might hear in the wild.

Signs of pregnancy are not immediately obvious in vixens; the size and shape of the mother are only slightly altered by the tiny unborn

12

The first indications of Vicky's pregnancy were the changes in her usually invisible teats

cubs. By March, however, Vicky's appetite had increased. The first sure indication came a short while before the birth as, when a vixen is within days of cubbing, the fur around her teats becomes bare and the teats themselves (usually pale and almost invisible) begin to grow bright pink and prominent.

Around this time, Jacky became very attentive. He would follow Vicky almost everywhere, sleeping right beside her both inside her den and outside on the grass, and bringing her presents of food and toys. Jacky's intentions were unquestionably worthy but of the many injuries to new-born cubs in the wild – I have seen a variety of cases, from young adults with stumps for tails to vixens emerging from their dens with litters of only two or three – are most possibly caused by over-protective parents. Our decision to separate the two foxes before the birth met with little disapproval on their part: the sudden

Jacky, the expectant father, nestling up to and protecting Vicky

absence of her mate did not worry Vicky in the least, while Jacky, perhaps surprisingly, appeared just as unconcerned to be kept away from the mother of his cubs.

We made an insulated wooden box and placed it inside a small poultry house in the middle of a large grass pen, hoping that this would provide the most suitable environment for the confinement. Vicky took to it straight away. With the mother so relaxed, healthy and happy, everything looked to be going more smoothly than we would have dared imagine. The next day, I did the usual morning round, checking on all of the foxes. As I neared the little wooden house, I could hear plaintive cries coming from underneath. Vicky had dug a narrow shallow tunnel beneath the box and appeared unable to move. Although the pleasure she showed at my lifting the house to free her was as lively as ever, it was clear that she wanted to give birth in a more natural den.

Another of our vixens, Sheba, had years before dug herself a small underground den in the adjacent pen. The hole was a shallow structure, about six feet in length with a short fork at the end. As soon as the door

Vicky greets a visiting fallow deer with interest

of Sheba's pen was opened, Vicky trotted straight over to the den and disappeared. With the month having been reasonably mild thus far, the insulation of the wooden box appeared to have been an unnecessary precaution; Sheba's den, meeting the basic needs of Vicky's instincts and bringing the conditions a step nearer to those she would have had in the wild, appeared to be an even more satisfactory arrangement.

However, the next day saw a sudden change in the weather. The morning was bitterly cold, with a strong north wind blowing directly down the hole. Against the sound of these gusts, I could make out faint squeaks coming from the den. Vicky had given birth, but she and her new-born cubs remained out of sight in the hole. There was no way to ensure that they were all right. All we could do was leave them in the cold and wait.

The following day brought even worse weather: stronger wind, but now rain as well. Some time in the afternoon, Vicky emerged, covered in wet yellow clay. She was carrying a cub. It would, had all been well,

Anxious Jacky guards the mother-to-be, ready for action if necessary

have been too early for her to be moving the cubs; this was a sign that the conditions were causing both mother and cubs considerable distress. Yet Vicky was determined that even this was preferable to an entirely artificial habitat: when I offered her a house in the next run, she showed no interest at all, merely carrying her cub back down into the sodden earth.

Although we were resigned to our inability simply to go in and get the cubs, we saw that if Vicky brought them out as she had before, there might be a possibility of our taking them from her. By way of preparation, a soft blanket was placed inside a cardboard box, which was in turn placed on an electric heating pad in our living-room. When Vicky next appeared carrying a cub, I reached gently to remove it from her mouth; she offered no resistance, allowing me to take the new-born as if I were a member of the family.

Tiny Tessa, the only surviving cub in Vicky's litter, takes to her bottle

We carried the cub home, cleaned the damp soil from its coat, and attempted to feed it. We used an 8 ml syringe containing a mixture of Lactol, a pinch of glucose and a little calcium, together with some warm water. With patience and painstaking care, we managed to insert the syringe into the side of the cub's tiny mouth. After the syringe was empty, the cub was placed in the warm box where it quickly fell asleep. At bedtime, everything needed for a night-time

Tessa with Rita Tushingham

feed, including a vacuum flask of hot water and, of course, dear little Tessa, were taken upstairs and placed beside our bed. Faint cries woke us once each night; both the cub's understanding of its environment and its hearing were developed enough for the cries to stop immediately at the sound of the meal being prepared. At this time, the cub weighed just 3½ oz.

As far as we knew, this was only the first of Vicky's cubs that we could help. Our concern for the rest of the litter persisted throughout the day and night after this first rescue. As I approached Vicky the following morning, she was carrying a black object in her mouth. I hoped that we might be able to take a second cub from her just as we had the first, but as I neared I saw that the object was not one cub but three. All were very weak, probably suffering from hypothermia, and there was nothing we could do to save them. I brought the three cubs home but they were too weak to drink milk. We were greatly saddened that they had passed the point of no return. The most likely explanation for all the difficulties of the birth is that, probably in spite of Vicky's best attempts, the extreme cold and damp overcame the cubs' instinct to be suckled; in the very conditions when nourishment was most important, the new-born cubs received none. Of the entire litter, only the one rescued cub survived, and continued to survive in our care. We named her Tessa.

2   Tessa

Tessa was born with a black coat and a blunt, rounded head. She grew remarkably quickly and after only a few days was able to drink from a bottle fitted with a premature-baby teat, donated by a local hospital. The colour of her nose changed from pink to black within a week. After three weeks, her eyes began to open and she began to walk, unsteadily at first. Her hind legs were considerably weaker than her front legs – a natural impediment which prevents cubs born in the wild from emerging into the outside world before they are five or six weeks old, by which time they are active and alert.

Tessa, like her mother Vicky zealously guards her beloved toys

At three and a half weeks, Tessa was still bottle fed every three hours or so. After each meal she was encouraged to walk around the living-room floor. Soon she could be persuaded to lap from a saucer, her first step in the process of weaning. Before long, she had moved on to Heinz baby food for 3–6 month-olds. (Egg and Bacon Breakfast proved to be her favourite.) She stayed in the same cardboard box used immediately after her rescue. This now sat on a desk and was fitted with a wire-netting top to prevent her climbing out. At this stage of her cubhood, she would become very excited when we picked her up at feeding time; her small tail would wag and she would breathe 'hah-hah-hah' as a kind of greeting.

Tessa with her favourite toy

We could not of course match the care Tessa would have received had she been born and survived in the wild. Having never been suckled by Vicky, she missed out on both the perfect nourishment for a fox cub and certain antibodies she would now never receive. We were unable to clean Tessa as thoroughly as her mother might have. This led, after a few weeks, to a kind of nappy rash, but as is often the case, human remedies provided the answer: the ailment went away as easily as it had appeared after the application of a lotion manufactured for babies. Of all the minor advantages of being in human care, it is the human toy which provides the greatest comfort for our foxes. Each tends to have his or her favourite, over which it displays unmistakably childlike possessiveness. Vicky had been known to hide her playthings under her bedding when two new cubs arrived for a brief stay. Even at this early age, Tessa showed herself to have the same inclinations. When she was let out to play in the living-room, she would scamper straight over to the selection of toys and pick one out to push and pull, shake and toss. When she grew tired of playing, she would come to us and gently lick our fingers.

Tessa leaves bottle feeding well behind and eats her first solid meal of kitten food

At one month old, Tessa was fed some kitten-food, her first solid meal. The next day, after another meal and a walk around the room, she went into a frenzy as we tried to put her back in her box. For some minutes, she caught hold of her blanket and shook it frantically, refusing to let go. Previously, her droppings had consisted of small, dry yellow pellets. The solid meal meant that they would now be softer. Tessa's apparently erratic behaviour constituted a refusal to soil her bed – she was, in effect, demanding a latrine. She was now too old for the small cardboard box and needed a new home. The living-room with which she had become so familiar also had an airing cupboard. We cut a square four inch hole into a thicker cardboard box and placed the box on the electric heating pad (now used only every now and again) on the floor of the airing cupboard. The rest of the cupboard floor, right up to her hole in her box, was covered with newspapers which could be frequently replaced. The whole time she lived here, her sleeping box remained spotlessly clean. The new arrangement not only satisfied her standards of hygiene, but also

A contented Tessa settles down in her new airing cupboard den

enabled her still to eat and play in the living-room. Her contentment in this new den was unmistakable: after just two days, she ran for the first time.

3 Introductions

Tessa showing affection at just one month old

At five and a half weeks, Tessa seemed old enough to be taken outside and introduced to the other foxes – perhaps the most crucial aspect of her development. The separations which had taken place – of Jacky from Vicky, and then of Vicky from Tessa (without the cub having even been suckled) – meant that Tessa's parents were unlikely to recognize her as their own. Of all the foxes in our care, a 7-year-old elderly vixen called Sheba, who had been with us for five years, was the most likely to give Tessa a gentle, encouraging welcome. We had introduced a number of cubs to Sheba throughout her stay and each had seemed to bring out a distinctly maternal response. Tessa was no exception. She immediately took to Sheba, cuddling up to her as if she were her own mother. Wild cubs would not, at this stage, leave their den to play for very long, so we left the two together for only half an hour. This, however, was enough for Tessa to make real progress. The next day when we reunited them, Tessa began to hunt insects in the grass – a skill learned as quickly and as surely as if she had been in the wild.

Each day, Tessa was allowed to spend slightly longer playing outside in the morning. The Lactol in her diet was replaced with goat's milk – more easily digestible than cow's milk – and she became more and more active with each passing week. By the time she was eight weeks old, this energy often made her restless: she would leap frenetically

Eileen introduces Tessa to Sheba, who instantly bonds with her new foster mother

onto tables and chairs; at night in particular when we could hear her calling out to the other foxes amidst a series of thuds and clatters in the living-room. It was time for her to be moved outdoors permanently.

The bond Sheba had formed with Tessa had grown stronger with each visit, and it seemed sensible for them to share a den, allowing Sheba's tendency to mother Tessa to develop more naturally in its own time. We took Tessa out to play with Sheba as usual, but instead of bringing her back after a while, we allowed her to stay, curious to see if they would make a home together. As was the layout of most of the foxes' pens, Sheba's kennel was situated inside a small poultry house and consisted of a bed of molinia grass. *Molinia caurulea* is common beside forest tracks and has leaves up to three feet long. The leaves bleach white in winter and are easy to gather in the spring. Unlike ordinary hay and straw, this grass is not hollow-stemmed, and so will not harbour fleas. This was placed in a simple wooden box, measuring two foot square and nine inches high, with a seven-inch square entrance hole and a wooden lid. That night, the two foxes happily shared Sheba's bed of grass. The arrangement suited them both and eventually lasted for several months.

Around the time she was moved outdoors, she was looking a little more like an adult fox, although her fur retained its woolly undercoat. Her diet was now beginning more closely to resemble that of the other foxes. The fox is perhaps the truest omnivore; wild foxes eat almost anything – blackberries, apples, worms, fungi, rodents, rabbits, birds and most dead or dying wildlife. Our kept foxes have a slightly more artificial, but equally varied diet: dog and cat-food, from tinned meat to biscuits and doggy chocolate drops; many human products, such as muesli (often mixed with other cereal, raw eggs and raisins), cheese, fruit, nuts, chicken drumsticks, as well as leftovers and other scraps; raw bones (cooked bones are not digested and might cause a blockage and cooked poultry bones could splinter). We also gave them any squirrels or rabbits found killed on the road or from the butchers, frozen and then thawed so as to kill off any mites still on the fur. The main chicken hatcheries, inevitably producing as many unwanted cockerels as saleable pullets, kill and dispose of many bags full of dead day-old chicks. As

Motherly Sheba happily shares her bed of grass with the lively Tessa

more wildlife rescue centres have been established, the nutritional value of these poor chicks has been recognized (they are particularly rich in calcium). For recovering birds and mammals, from hawks and owls to stoats, polecats, badgers and foxes, they provide a most balanced form of nourishment. In addition to the above scraps, the foxes in our care consume about half a dozen sacks of these chicks every month. Very soon after joining Sheba, Tessa happily ate her first day-old chick. It was interesting to note that the chicks were always eaten head first which would have been a quick death should they have been alive.

Throughout these early stages of her development, Tessa benefited tremendously from the company of a cub of approximately her own age. Earlier in the year, before Tessa's birth, two police constables came to our door with a tiny dog fox they had found by the roadside. It was a bitterly cold morning and the WPC was carrying the cub tucked into her blouse to keep it warm. His eyes were open, which meant he was at least three weeks old, but his size made him look younger. I took him upstairs where Eileen snuggled him up with her in bed; within five minutes he was fast asleep. We named him Robbie, after Sir Robert Peel, a token of gratitude to his rescuers.

The growing Tessa sprawls out on the grass with me

Little Robbie, who was rescued from the roadside by the police, makes his first photo-call

We introduced Robbie to Tessa shortly after she had moved out into Sheba's den. Though he was a little older than Tessa, and slightly bigger, they treated one another as peers, almost as if they had been part of the same litter. Their meeting caused them both great excitement and led a few weeks later, to an enormous amount of chasing and playing; Tessa would hide, under branches and bushes, and Robbie would jump high over her. Robbie was let in with Tessa every morning and evening. Their enjoyment of each other's company heightened with every day, as though they were a couple of childhood friends.

From a nearby pen, Vicky was also introduced to Tessa. Neither fox showed any awareness that they were mother and daughter. Whereas Sheba had been extremely patient with Tessa's rather rough playfulness, allowing her tail, ears and legs to be tweaked and pulled, Vicky

29

Opposite – Robbie larks about, happily jumping over Tessa – his new playmate

did not respond so generously to this treatment, and reciprocated vigorously at first. Vicky was returned to her own pen after a short while and taken back to Tessa daily. They were allowed to spend a longer stretch of time together each day, and before long they began to play together quite peacefully, but there was never any sign that they might, even unwittingly, re-establish their mother-daughter relationship.

Tessa's father, Jacky, was a much heavier fox; if Tessa had played with him at a very early age, the difference in their sizes would have put her at some risk. For some weeks we allowed them to meet from either side of a weldmesh wire partition, allowing them to become familiar with each other, but not to play. By August, Tessa was almost four months old. She was half-grown, strong and active, and capable of protecting herself from any potential accidental harm. When Jacky was first let into Sheba's pen, he seemed to be intrigued by this new, fuller contact with Tessa. Tessa was no less playful than before, pulling him roughly about. His response lay somewhere in between Sheba's tolerance and Vicky's retaliation: he would bear with the cub contentedly for some time, but whenever her games grew a little too strenuous, he would give an authoritative growl as a firm, mild warning. Tessa always obeyed, backing off immediately, and usually turning her attention to Sheba, whose patience was tested repeatedly but never waned. After this first meeting, Jacky was allowed to enter their pen whenever he fancied. Within days, their interaction became considerably more relaxed. Jacky often settled to grooming Tessa; occasionally, Tessa and Sheba together groomed Jacky. Either way, all three seemed quietly blissful. Again, there was no indication that Jacky might have been aware of his natural relationship with Tessa, but in the way that his presence and authority helped to calm her down, he came to play as important a part in her developing maturity as he might have done in the wild. Customarily, foxes are conscientious fathers. They bring food to the den while the cubs are small and hidden underground. Later, they will hide food many yards away for the vixen to collect, and when

31

the cubs grow older they will also collect from these sites. Well into the autumn, they will still pass food to the vixen and cubs should they meet in the area.

Tessa, being mothered by Sheba and Vicky

4   Visitors

We have never really encouraged people to visit our sanctuary; there always seems to be too much to do without the additional task of having to look after guests. However, word of the foxes at our cottage spread more quickly than I could have imagined and more broadly than I could, even now, begin to account for. During the year of Tessa's birth, we received around 170 families and other parties (comprising over 500 individuals) from as far as Russia, America, South Africa, New Zealand and even the South Pacific. There were

Tessa entertaining one of the hundreds of people who visited Badger Cottage

also visitors from all over Britain, people whose interests in wildlife ranged from passing curiosity to professional research – from stars of stage and screen to academics, photography students and television producers, as well as members of parliament looking for first-hand evidence to support their views against fox-hunting.

Summer brought the greatest number of visitors, August and September being the busiest months, particularly as many people were holidaying in the New Forest. All of the foxes seemed to love this opportunity for meeting and playing with strangers. Tessa, though still far from fully grown, had become an even-tempered young vixen who would joyfully run up to visitors, introducing herself with a nose-to-nose greeting. She jumped on backs, pulled clothes and chewed shoe-laces. She, along with several of the other foxes, had a particular fondness for leather, tossing handbags and tugging relentlessly at shoes. Before long, one or two had even learned deftly to unfasten watch straps. Local visits often included children – some researching for school projects, others as part of cub scout and brownie groups on outings, and also many children for whom the foxes' company had

Sheba welcomes an 11-month old baby with her friendly nose-to-nose greeting

a degree of therapeutic value. On one occasion, a class of children with severe learning difficulties crouched in a row on the grass while Sheba leapt from back to back right to the end. Sheba noticed one boy sitting apart from the others; she went over to him and looked into his face for some time. The boy, who had been silent all day and was, according to his teacher, generally uncommunicative, grew immediately less reserved. By the time the children were leaving, he was more talkative than any of them. Animals see beyond handicaps in a way that people only try to, and many show an instinctive understanding of human behaviour. Foxes are no exception.

Tessa chewing a visitor's shoe-lace!

The number of visitors increased as people got to know of our unusual 'guests'. We were always interested in the thank-you letters that we often received following a visit, for these gave an insight into the reactions of people whose eyes had been opened to the true nature of these special animals.

Sheba enjoying the attentions of some of the many school parties who came to visit our foxes each year

Sheba, especially happy with her new young friends

Here are a few extracts from some of those letters:

'It was throat-thumping for us to be able to engage in actually stroking such beautiful and friendly animals'.

'It was a marvellous experience for all of us and especially for the boys who haven't stopped talking about it since'.

'I had not fully realized what beautiful creatures foxes are, it has certainly reinforced my will to try and put an end to the barbaric hunting of foxes'.

Vicky cajoling a nun into some serious play!

'To look into the eyes of this animal you can see the very soul of Nature'.

'Reg and I were so thrilled to see your beautiful foxes, something that we never dreamed we would ever see. I couldn't sleep last night thinking about them'.

'It has been beyond my wildest dreams to actually hold a fox'.

'You could live a lifetime with them and still marvel at them'.

'It will be one of our treasured memories'.

'They must be the most wonderful creatures of our wildlife'.

'The fox is so misunderstood by man – he's great'.

'To have a fox as happy as Vicky only proves to me how important your work is'.

Sheba scent-marks Rachel's
showing her instant approval

Sheba discovers that enterta
visitors doesn't always inv
energetic leaping

Jacky, Sheba and Vicky attempt an alternative method of keeping visitors amused

'They are lovely, so gentle'.

'Russell is still on cloud nine being able to stroke a fox. Thank you so much for one of the most wonderful experiences we have ever had'.

'It was such a special evening, one that we will always remember'.

'Thank you so much for an experience of a lifetime'.

'It was a wonderful experience to be with the foxes, so unafraid and peaceful, and so obviously contented and responding to affection from you both'.

'None of us expected to see such wonderful rapport and trust as obviously exists between you and your much-loved foxes'.

'A privileged afternoon indeed and one we will all remember for a very long time to come'.

Sometimes a child who had been particularly impressed by their visit, would send a painting or drawing by way of thanks, a gesture that was always much appreciated.

Amber Forge.
Old Christchurch Rd
Everton.
Lymington.
Thursday.

Dear Mr and Mrs Ashby.
thankyou for Letting me play with
your Foxes also I have a fotograf for
you. I hope I can cum again if Sheba
has some cubs. Mummy is going to
get some prints of her fotografs for you
and send them wen they are ready.

love from

Claire
Taylor

5 Seasons: From Moulting to Breeding

During the summer, adult foxes begin to moult. By October, the coats start to look full and bushy, but it is not until November that the outer coats are fully grown. The undercoat is a highly effective insulator and the top coat is waterproof, so the fox is kept warm and dry throughout the winter months, even when curling up on frozen snow. The coats of cubs do not undergo this change during their first year but continue to grow consistently as their bodies increase in size. Their first moult, during their second year, has little adverse effect on the youngsters. As they age, however, the moults tend to induce lethargy and apathy, causing them to sleep more, particularly in the hot summer weather when moulting begins. In August the older foxes' coats become dull, ragged and patchy, which can easily be mistaken for mange-mite infection. By the end of the month the head and shoulders will be the first to complete the moult and will look fresh and bright. Improvement is very slow and they will carry on shedding their old coat for several more weeks. The older they get the more strain it is on their constitution. These are the inactive days of late summer, lying in the sun, moving to the shade and passing the time away. Then night-time is when they feed, play and have more energetic activity. The cooler weather of autumn understandably comes as some relief.

Lethargic Jacky shows his s[...]
moult

Foxes' main breeding season lasts from December to February. Wild foxes can be extremely vocal during this period. It is not always easy to tell which sounds are made by which sex, but for the most part, dog foxes give a distinctive low 'wo-wo-wo' call, while vixens' voices are generally higher-pitched, occasionally closer to screams than any other human sound. Foxes are extremely territorial all year round – on one occasion, when one of Sheba's fences was moved to give her more room, it took days of waiting and eventually throwing something for her to chase before she would cross the old boundary – but this predilection is accentuated in dog foxes during the breeding season. For most of the year, Jacky would squat like a vixen and deposit little scent. When the breeding season started, he began to cock his leg to scent-mark his fence. By the end of January, Jacky was following Tessa around, holding his tail straight up in the air.

We were in a dilemma. Jacky could not be left alone during the breeding season as he could have injured himself trying to break into another pen. Vicky had proved herself not to be a good mother, so Jacky could not stay with her. Eventually we decided to put Jacky in with Tessa, although we didn't want any more cubs, particularly from a daughter of Jacky. We hoped she would be too young to bear cubs.

With the beginning of breeding season, Jacky marks his territory

At this time, Tessa was only nine and a half months old. This seemed to us likely to be too young for any vixen to mate, not least one which had been fed and cared for artificially from such an early age. Although her happiness and well-being had been obvious throughout those nine months, we were sure that her mother's inability to suckle her and the nutrition which she inevitably missed out on at that time would have some effect on Tessa's ability to bear cubs in her first year, even if it meant her producing a litter of only one or two.

Towards the end of February, Tessa's appetite increased, the first good indication that she was in cub. We began to supplement her diet with Lactol, to help her to suckle her litter after the birth. At the same time, Jacky began to be more attentive to her. He would collect gifts – food and toys, sometimes together – and leave them near Tessa, and he would sleep beside her day and night. Whenever we approached, he bustled over, as if to protect her from any interference. A couple of weeks later, around the middle of March, Tessa was

Jacky and Tessa playing hard to get

Expectant mother Tessa awaiting the birth of her cubs

looking evenly rotund. I started to construct an insulated nesting box, consisting of an outer wooden case and a layer of polystyrene protected by hardboard. The outer measurement was twenty-four inches square by thirteen inches high, the inside about four inches smaller in each direction. The entrance hole was six inches square. The inside was filled with a bedding of wood shavings. The completed box was placed in Tessa's house in exchange for her normal sleeping box. Tessa went immediately to investigate, and settled down at once, scraping the floor as if making a bed.

On 21 March, Tessa had lost some hair around her teats, which had turned bright pink. With the birth only days away, Jack, and now Sheba as well, grew even more attentive, grooming Tessa constantly. We moved Sheba and Jacky into another pen, and, much like her mother only a year or so earlier, Tessa seemed not to mind being alone in her pen. She rested the following days, her tummy beginning to feel hot and tight. On 26 March, electricity men arrived to work up a pole only ten yards from her house. The men were sympathetic and managed to complete the job as quickly and as quietly as possible. Nevertheless, at one point the disturbance prompted her to leave her house and run anxiously around the pen for several minutes before returning, somewhat out of breath, and resting again.

The following morning, I found Tessa resting on top of her nursery box. When I placed a bowl of Lactol nearby, she leapt down and lapped it up voraciously. As she did so, I peered into the nursery and saw a heap of dark cubs. I was struck by their silence: there wasn't even the slightest murmur. I realized then that this was the natural state of a healthy new-born litter. My thoughts drifted to the previous year. The quiet contentment of Tessa's cubs put into perspective the cries that had come from the damp hole in the ground where Vicky had chosen to give birth. As lucky as Tessa and her cubs had been, and as much as we had now learned about how best to care for vixens in cub, it was difficult not to remember or regret.

Tessa's cubs, born in a warm dr den, at four days old

6   Tessa's Litter

Tessa had six cubs, which, considering her young age and the circumstances of her own birth, was a remarkable success, surpassing all our expectations. In addition to providing her with her usual diet, we continued to give her as much Lactol as she would drink so that there would be no chance of her being unable to feed all six mouths. The cubs remained quietly satisfied for days. At first, we were extremely cautious. Wild animals sometimes abandon or even eat their offspring if disturbed, and some domestic animals have been known to do the

The cubs, safe and sound at a week old

Tessa and her 2½-week-old cub
snuggle up to their mother, keep
ing warm

same if they believe that the litter is in danger. From the moment of
the birth, we were determined to ward off anything which could have
created the slightest disturbance. The reassurance we were looking
for came the day after the cubs were born: around midday, Tessa left
them for a few minutes and came to us to be made a fuss of. We
petted her and played with her, and she responded just as she used to
before and during her pregnancy.

After four days there was still barely a squeak to be heard from the
cubs. Their heads seemed to be growing more quickly than the rest of
their bodies and, though their eyes had not yet opened, they were
getting a little more active, climbing all over Tessa as she lay curled
around them. Over the course of these four days, it had become
increasingly obvious that, as far as her litter was concerned, Tessa was
treating us as though we were extended family. She showed us a

degree of trust remarkable even in view of our having rescued and reared her from the day of her birth. It took only these four days for us to be sure that she would not object to our handling the cubs.

On 1 April, the cub's fifth day, condensation began to form on the underside of the lid of Tessa's box. As the family were growing, the insulated enclosure was beginning to retain too much warmth. Tessa had now scraped the wood shavings up against the entrance, which, although it made the box even warmer, would have prevented any of the cubs from straying out onto the cold floor of the house as respite from the heat. I replaced the original lid with a plain wooden one and redistributed the shavings over the floor. By the seventh day, the cubs were generating enough of their own warmth for Tessa to leave them alone for longer periods. She had regained her previous strength and was becoming more and more playful, so we allowed Jacky to rejoin her for a while. It was a joyous reunion, Tessa dashing around after Jacky, trying to take his legs away from under him. After about ten minutes, they began to look tired and soon happily went their separate ways.

ostling for space, Tessa and her
½-week-old cubs

After two weeks, we were able to sex the cubs: there were three vixens (including by far the smallest of the litter) and three dog cubs. Before long, their eyes began to open slowly, tiny slits of brightness beginning to show on day fifteen. The next day, which was very warm, Tessa brought them out of the box. She picked up each by its head (rather than by the scruff of its neck – a technique peculiar to her) and when they were all outside, she suckled them on the floor for the first time. Foxes' instincts towards their homes are dominated by attention to detail and by an overwhelming concern for cleanliness. Tessa kept her cubs and their den spotless. As little as two weeks after the birth, we had seen Tessa move three cubs outside the box so that she could scrape at and re-arrange the wood shavings, before taking them back in to join the others. When, two and a half weeks after they had been born, Tessa was suckling them on the floor, one of the cubs began to cry. Tessa interpreted the sound at once: she quickly bent round, cleaning away the water passing from the cub's rear and disposing of the black slug-like dropping that appeared. Looking on, I was again reminded of Tessa's own infancy, of her refusal to soil her first home. Tessa's cubs seemed to benefit from the maternal care and understanding that all cubs should have, even though Tessa herself had not been so fortunate.

As the photographs show, the cubs grew at a tremendous rate. Tessa's appetite was increasing, as was her thirst for water and milk; also, we noticed that she moved her mouth around, as if masticating, when she returned to the litter. This suggested that she was now supplementing their milk with regurgitated, partially digested food, just as vixens do in the wild. Soon after they were three weeks old, Tessa began to present the cubs with day-old chicks. They were not yet old enough to eat the chicks, but they played with them and sucked them, developing an early familiarity with and a taste for a staple element of their future diet.

At this stage of their development, the cubs were becoming considerably more active. They still spent much of their time asleep, but, increasingly, thumps and bumps could be heard from their box, along

Opposite – The cubs emerge into the outside world of the pen, temporarily leaving the den's warmth and safety

with excited cries as they played together. It seemed likely that it would be only a matter of days before they wandered out of their box. They were, compared to the wild animals in the New Forest surrounding their enclosure, still very small; it was all too easy to imagine one of the cubs wandering too far out onto the grass, offering itself as easy, isolated prey for a crow or magpie to swoop down and attack. All our fox pens, except the first one, are enclosed by a six-foot high, two-inch square weldmesh fence, with an overhang on the inward side of each pen, about eighteen inches wide, made of two-inch wire netting. On the ground two-foot square paving slabs are placed against the fence to discourage digging out.

Tessa's pen is eighteen yards by ten yards, not covered over of course, so that both crows and magpies have been seen scavenging in the pen, and twice a buzzard has been seen flying from the enclosures. Crows in particular are well known for pecking the eyes out of new-born lambs, so we thought that our tiny cubs might be in danger. We built a kind of short, wooden playpen against their house. It was high enough to prevent a cub from climbing out, but small enough so as not to present Tessa with any real obstacle.

At around this time, between three and four weeks after their birth, one vixen cub, the smallest of the litter, was not growing as quickly as the others. Her general demeanour seemed, in comparison to that of the other cubs, unhealthy. Indeed, as the others grew, she appeared to be weakening. After a day or two of observing her deterioration, we brought her indoors and hoped that she might benefit from our own intensive, human care. Despite all our efforts, the cub died less than twenty-four hours after we had attempted to rescue her. We examined her closely after rigor mortis had set in and found that her neck had been broken. The cause of this was not immediately apparent but, with hindsight, it seems most likely to have been the result of Tessa's picking her cubs up by the head rather than by the scruff. Reasons for Tessa's having adopted this method of carrying her young are really anybody's guess. It could have been the result of her not having had a mother herself and so of having never been picked

Tessa keeps careful watch over her new family – the fence might keep the cubs inside, but it cannot prevent attack from magpies and crows

up by another fox, or perhaps it was down to her youth, or simply her character. Whatever the explanation, it was only this cub, always the smallest and the weakest of the litter, which suffered as a result.

In the fourth week following the cubs' birth, Tessa seemed, for the first time, to be encouraging them to leave the den. To begin with, she placed a day-old chick in the playpen and buried another nearby. Later, in a more endearing – if perhaps slightly less convincing – attempt to entice them out with food, she stood a little distance from the house and gave a soft call, reminiscent of a clucking hen. The cubs remained reluctant to take such a big step. It was not until four days later that they first emerged: two cubs wandered unsteadily about the playpen, and were promptly picked up and carried home by their mother.

From then on, all of the cubs quickly became more adventurous. They wandered uncertainly but bravely around the pen, watched by Tessa at all times. Once a cub seemed suddenly to grow confused and momentarily lost only a short distance from the den. Rather than simply picking it up, Tessa gently nudged her nose against first one side of the cub and then the other, and so on until she had guided it

Tessa gives her cub a highly nutritious chick to eat

all the way back to the entrance of the house. As the cubs spent more time out of the den, so Tessa began to spend a little more time further away from them. When they were one month old, she suckled them on top of the box and began to sleep apart from them, in the nearby house of an adjoining pen. The cubs' eyesight was still very poor, but their senses of hearing and smell were sharp enough to compensate. Tessa appeared to watch contentedly as they came out to enjoy the grass and scuttled back at the slightest strange sound.

The cubs continued to grow at a prodigious rate. Less than two weeks after the installation of the playpen, the cubs were large and agile enough to attempt to climb over. One bold vixen succeeded, tumbling to the ground outside before we lifted the pen a few inches and Tessa gave her a firm and authoritative push back inside. Mindful of the danger of a cub climbing out at night unnoticed by Tessa, we removed the pen, allowing the litter a much greater level of freedom. The next day, two cubs ventured into the adjacent run where Tessa was keeping watch. One of them trotted over to Vicky who was looking through the fence from her run with great interest. The cub wagged its tail and greeted her, but Tessa, apparently thinking this too

bold, gave a short growl and carried the truant briskly back to its nursery. That night, Tessa and one of the cubs slept together in the house next door. Later on, two more cubs moved into this pen with her, and wandered over to greet Vicky, this time with their mother's approval.

At six weeks old, the cubs were still being suckled outside. Tessa's udders were shrinking discernibly and she began to suckle them less, instead burying food for them to find. They would search the grass for food whenever they tired of their increasingly vigorous play, and at six and a half weeks old, they began to develop their technique of hunting insects – leaping up about two feet into the air before pouncing down sharply. A surer supply of food came from Jacky who began to push day-old chicks through the dividing wire for them to eat. For months afterwards, he always passed food to the cubs before eating anything himself. This behaviour was, perhaps, less paternal than it might seem: in the wild, adult foxes pass food to any youngster that begs for it, right up to the breeding season of their first year. Occasionally, this instinctive co-operation stretches further than the inherent concern for the young. Once after dark, I noticed Sheba

Preceding page – Bliss! Tess suckling her 6-week-old cubs

Attending to the happy family when the cubs are eight weeks old

Concerned Jacky passes a chick to a cub through the fence

pawing noisily at her wire fence. As I approached, a wild fox ran away and there, partly pushed through the weldmesh, was a dead bat. Foxes' camaraderie, their general level of concern for each other, particularly with regard to their feeding habits, is perhaps surprising to those with little experience of their behaviour. It is, however, entirely consistent with the rest of their character.

Sheba's relationship with Tessa's litter offered, above all, insight into the extent to which the last year had aged her. Her instinctively maternal response to cubs which were not her own was still discernible, just as it had been twelve months earlier with Tessa, but she was now limited by her unmistakable and gradually increasing weariness. Her first meeting with the cubs was marked by wagging tails, excited play and palpable joy. After a few days, however, she seemed to find them a little too boisterous. She left them from time to time, getting away from the relentless tail and ear pulling which characterized their play. Yet Sheba always returned at night – she still loved to sleep near them.

Tessa introducing Sheba to
boisterous cubs

By the end of June, the cubs stopped using the box in which they were born. By July, they were nearly half-grown, lanky and foxy-looking, but still on occasion displaying a fair amount of naiveté. At this stage, their innocence stemmed primarily from their youth, but the question of how much of their naiveté remained would be an important issue as they grew into adulthood. As the months passed, on through Tessa's unusually early moult – due to the strain of giving birth – the cubs grew healthily and happily throughout the next winter without problems. By the following March, they were fully grown. We faced the decision of whether or not to release them into the wild.

The life expectancy of the fox has decreased rapidly in recent years: the average age of the country fox is now as little as between twelve and eighteen months. With freedom comes hunger, disease, accident and persecution. Each of these dangers is severe enough for those foxes born into such conditions. For those who were born and bred in captivity, who have yet to develop the skills and the resilience necessary for survival in the wild, and whose very search for an empty territory might fail – forcing them to die before their struggle has even begun – the hazards are formidable. If health and safety were the only criteria, no fox would ever leave our sanctuary. Nor is it merely a question of happiness: the eyes and the actions of the foxes in our care attest to their joy and contentment. Nonetheless, the fact remains that the fox is not a domestic animal. The wilderness is its true home. The beauty of wildlife lies primarily in its being wild.

Tragically, many cubs become road casualties, and only a few are as lucky as Robbie

Opposite – It is impossib
warn Tessa's cubs of the da
of the wild

7   Suzie

The only way to balance these factors in making a decision to release a fox is to take each case on its individual merits. One fox in particular, however, has helped us to understand the more general issues involved. When she was just a week or so old, eyes still tightly closed, Suzie was found in a Hertfordshire field by a man out walking his dog. He left her for an hour, hoping that her mother would come and take her back to her earth, but the cub was still in exactly the same spot when he returned. He took her home where he and his family (including two young boys) kept her as a pet for as long as they could. After five weeks of rearing the cub, giving her sustenance, care, attention and, in the form of the two boys, particularly energetic playmates, the family were no longer able to provide suitable accommodation for the growing stray. She was given a temporary home at a wildlife hospital near the New Forest. There, she began to become accustomed to the attentions of the hospital's many visitors. She hated to see them go and would climb the weldmesh of her pen in disappointment as they left. By the time she came to us on 10 June 1994, climbing had become part of her play, an activity like any other. Foxes are all usually capable of climbing, but all of the other foxes we have looked after climbed very rarely, only when frightened or disturbed. Suzie, on the other hand, as soon as she noticed our presence, would run to one end of her pen, climb to the top of the weldmesh fence, jump to the ground, then race excitedly to the other end of her run to climb the fence again, before jumping onto our backs and shoulders to pull our hair.

Suzie climbing up and 'mugging' a visitor

Perhaps because of the young boys at her first home, Suzie was considerably more boisterous than the foxes we were used to. For some weeks, she was allowed to roam freely between all of the grass pens, in the company of the other foxes. She began to sleep in the same house as Jacky, who, as with Tessa, would give an effective little growl if he became annoyed by Suzie's attentions; like Tessa, she would back off at once. This combination, of freedom and space and the opportunity to interact with other foxes – all of which was new to her – seemed to calm her down a little. Being around people still excited her; sometimes she tugged furiously at our arms and legs and we did our best not to respond, the sort of approach that one might bring to a child looking for attention. Eventually, her physical displays of friendship grew less vigorous, but her propensity for climbing never waned.

Suzie's first year with us was healthy, happy and increasingly peaceful. She developed from an excitable cub into a fully grown vixen, and her progress continued throughout the following winter and spring. Then, one morning in May, Suzie could not be found anywhere. We searched all the runs and inspected all the fences: there was no sign

Suzie shows some distinctly human affection by giving a kiss

of her presence and no obvious route for her escape. She seemed simply to have disappeared. The next morning, we found her happily asleep, back in her favourite house.

Suzie had found her own way of having the best of both worlds – reaping the benefits of captivity while enjoying the freedom and the will of the wild. Almost every day, she spent all day resting in her house before leaving her pen in the evening. It became easy to watch her way out: she climbed the weldmesh fence to the top and, with one paw, pulled the overhang down towards her; using both her paws, she vaulted on top and walked along the wire overhang as though it were a solid path; then she simply jumped down to the ground. She returned in the same manner, and would be safely back in her pen before the end of each night. Foxes' lives are usually divided into two. Day is the rest time and night the hunting and feeding time. So the fox is nocturnal out of necessity as it is easier to catch prey at night. But when they have to feed cubs, hunting happens day and night, which is why I was able to film a vixen catching a rabbit in bright morning light. Wild foxes in situations with little or no disturbance, live mostly above ground, except in bad weather or at breeding time. Suzie still comes to our back door even on a rainy night. She looks very wet but her undercoat keeps her dry against the skin.

Suzie became adept at climbing out of her pen and was therefore able to reap the benefits of captivity *and* enjoy the freedom of the wild

Her double life continued into the autumn. In October, when the fallow deer rut, we saw Suzie just before dark, boldly approaching some antlered fallow bucks, coming a little too close to them, almost appearing to tease them. The next morning, she was back in her box as usual, but was seriously injured. Her groin was badly damaged and one hind leg hung down limp and useless, making it extremely difficult for her to walk. She was suffering from shock, and for four days she drank only

Opposite – Suzie following her excellent recovery from some terrible injuries

66

water and ate nothing. On the fifth day after her injury, she ate part of a day-old chick. From then on, antibiotics were administered by being injected into her food. Soon she was able to bend her hind leg slightly when she squatted, dispelling fears of a break or dislocation.

Given the care and the rest, foxes are able to recover fully – and often extremely rapidly – from the most appalling injuries. Soon after Tessa's birth, her mother, Vicky, somehow had her claw and pad ripped away; her foot needed dressing with antibiotics for weeks, but, remarkably, both her pad and claw grew back and (aside from a slight curve in the claw) her foot returned to normal. One feeder of wild foxes has told us that one of her regular visitors arrived one evening with her head covered in blood. The fox had a large hole on one side of its skull and a smaller one exactly opposite, almost certainly the result of a bullet passing right through. It was even possible to see daylight from one hole through to the other. A few weeks later, without the help of a vet and despite the difficulties of continuing to survive in the wild, the wound had healed completely and could barely be seen.

Lady of leisure: Suzie taki[ng a] well deserved rest

Just three days after her first dose of antibiotics, Suzie, still walking on only three legs, decided to leave her pen once again. Her determination to retain her freedom despite her needing to be cared for was remarkable, so great that there was certainly some risk of her either exacerbating her injuries, or even suffering a new one in her attempts to scale the fences in this condition. Therefore I separated one of the enclosures and cut a small hole in the wire netting for her to use as an entrance, essentially allowing her to live like a wild fox, but with food and a comfortable house for her at ground level. It took her some time to find this entrance and to begin to feed regularly in this new run. Even then, she insisted occasionally on climbing the fence to join the other foxes, her old companions.

Within a few weeks, Suzie had recovered completely and was beginning to spend more time away from the pens. As winter drew in, though we continued to leave her food and she continued to take it at night, we rarely saw her at all. Her previous determination to leave every evening, whatever the obstacles, and her increasing absence during the breeding season seemed to suggest that she had found a wild mate. A few weeks later, in the middle of March, I noticed in the early morning light that Suzie's teats were swollen: she had given birth. It was not until a whole month later, from the kitchen window, we saw her on the natural badger sett in the corner of our field, with several small cubs. A few days later, as I waited for an opportunity to photograph the litter, Suzie emerged from the sett, followed by six cubs. Within a few minutes, all were happily being suckled, but it was clear that Suzie had the signs of a mange-mite infection. Mange is easily cured – just ½ml of *Ivomec* put in the fox's food, once a week for three weeks – but the remedy cannot be given to lactating animals. She had to suffer the mange until we were sure that the cubs were feeding largely on solid food. Eventually we found her in one of the pens, obviously in trouble. She approached us with a series of moanful little cries; mange covered several parts of her body, as well as surrounding her half-closed eyes. We gave her the medicine, syringed into the mouth of a chick. The cubs had almost certainly caught the

infection from their mother, so several similarly treated chicks were
placed in Suzie's house – she was very likely to feed them to the cubs.
Fortunately, we have since discovered a much gentler, and equally
effective, treatment for mange. We simply put four or five drops of a
homeopathic remedy (ARSEN/ALB SULPH.30) in their food for
fourteen days. This is much safer than *Ivomec*, a drug usually used on
cattle to rid them of warble fly larvae and other parasites.

Suzie hunted naturally for her cubs, but we continued to supplement their diet. Throughout the summer, chicks were left in her
house several times a day, and she would take big mouthfuls down to
the sett and quietly call the litter. They were so well fed that they did
not always respond. As the weeks passed, we saw less and less of

Despite their mother's visits, Suzie's cubs were wild and kept their distance, preferring their badger sett home

Suzie. When she did come to the cottage, she was still as happy to interact with us as she had been during her stay.

Having been rescued as a tiny cub, Suzie treated humans as one of her family and would put her life at risk to protect us as well as her cubs. All vixens will bark at any sign of danger when her cubs are in the open causing them to bolt back home. One early Autumn evening in 1996 I was at the bottom of our field when an invisible fox started to give alarm barks. I recognized Suzie's voice. A fox's bark is a sharp, low-pitched scream. The hedge is wide and thick and I called 'Suzie, Suzie, Suzie', and in a little while she came through the hedge, still barking at intervals. She led the way along the hedge, obviously very worried, and then she stopped at a gap, where I could see through on to our neighbours' land. A huge, long-haired German Shepherd dog stood looking menacingly at brave Suzie. Suzie stood still. At intervals she would lunge forward and bark, until I growled at the dog thus telling it to be off – it immediately turned tail, followed by Suzie who went, still barking on to our neighbour's land. A minute later all went quiet.

I walked up the field towards home pondering just how brave she had been and hoping she was safe. Half-way back, I glanced down and there walking beside me was a very proud little vixen. She gazed up at me, very pleased with herself, having seen the dog off. How else would she show her love and loyalty? The whole episode gave us a wonderful insight into the special character of foxes. Never before had Suzie walked beside me to our cottage. This to her was a special occasion.

Her cubs, however, were wild and would not tolerate people nearby. They became increasingly nocturnal. As the days shortened, we saw them only after dark, when the food we left out for them enticed them near our outside light. By late autumn, we still saw four of them every now and again, and these four were in fine condition; Suzie herself was beginning to develop a beautiful winter coat. We would never even have considered attempting to tame the cubs, but this did not prevent us from being able to help them.

Suzie achieved a unique balance between captivity and the wild. The strength of her will to find freedom was extraordinary, yet clearly she thought of our cottage as her home. Perhaps the most remarkable

Opposite – Joey, one of Tes cubs, looking wistful

Suzie and her cubs a month la enjoying their freedom

element of her story is that when she was first injured, she somehow managed successfully to negotiate the fence and the overhang to get back *into* her pen. Without our care, she might never have recovered from those injuries; and without the mange remedy and the food we provided, her wild cubs might never have survived their infancy. But the wilderness remains their and their mother's rightful home. In many ways, we treat our foxes as pets; in many ways, even if only temporarily, they respond as pets. But all we really do is provide a sanctuary, the time and the place to assist these wild animals when they need assistance, and to help them to live free and natural lives as soon as they are able.

8   Sandy, Joey and Timmy

In the wild, dog cubs tend to move away from their earth before their first year is out, leaving the vixen cubs behind to help rear their mother's next litter in the spring. In May 1992, when Tessa's cubs were fourteen months old, we decided to set free her three dog cubs – Sandy, Joey and Timmy. This was considerably later than they might have left a natural den, but May is by far the best time of year to release cubs born into captivity: though there is generally more road traffic in the summer, wild food is at its most plentiful and, above all, there is no fox-hunting during May so there is no risk from huntsmen or their hounds. There were still many dangers ahead of them, but we knew that if they did get hurt, they would probably return to the sanctuary of their own accord. On 5 May, the forecast promising good weather for the next few days, we fed all three of them particularly well in the evening and left the pen door open after midnight. Each evening, their usual rations were placed in their house and leftovers were removed the next day. This continued until little if any food was taken and they appeared no longer to need any more help.

Joey, the most attached of the three to his first home, returned to the cottage the morning after his release, feeding in his old run and spending the day in his sleeping box. Later, he was chased and almost caught by a neighbour's Doberman, but he managed to flee safely back to our field. This seemed to be enough to convince him that he

was safe at home: he slept in his old pen all day every day for the next fortnight. Sandy, too, soon returned. He was back, sitting on the lawn, three days after his release. Occasionally he would approach us, sometimes to take a little food that we offered him, sometimes just for affection.

The cubs' new-found freedom enabled them to learn more about the animals which shared their surroundings. Although at odds with the generally perceived image of the fox as a solitary creature, this awareness of and interest in their neighbours has always been one of their more striking characteristics. When observed in a domestic environment, they seem keen to interact with domestic animals, especially cats. One correspondent from Cyprus – where the authorities pay the equivalent of £1 for every dead fox brought to them – has sent us letters and photographs detailing the friendship between a wild fox and several semi-wild cats, involving almost as much play as foxes' relationships with each other. After their release, Sandy and Joey took every opportunity to indulge the curiosity they had always had for our two pet cats. One of the cats, Lucy, was in the habit of going out onto the field to wait for the wild foxes to arrive, and then

Preceding page – Sandy, Tessa and Darky together at Badger Cottage

Marcel and Rufus in Cyprus proving that friendship between a wild fox and a semi-wild cat is possible

Our cat, Lucy, indulging in her unusual pastime of observing the wild foxes around our land

watching them eat the scraps we had put down. She, in particular, enjoyed the company of Sandy and Joey. Each would approach her, tentatively and clearly intrigued. Often she would reciprocate their interest, and other times she would remain indifferent; but when she did not like their attention she never hesitated to scare them away.

Sandy seemed to be adapting well, sleeping in his old home most days and going out every night. A couple of weeks after his release, he showed real signs of his growing independence as he squabbled with some wild foxes in the field. The next day, half a mile away from Badger Cottage, he was seen approaching a neighbour's cat. The neighbour assumed that the cat was in danger and shot and killed Sandy.

Joey was a little more fortunate. He still returned every day, apparently as much to play with the cats as to rest in his home. As time passed, less and less food was being taken from his pen and he began to feed with the other wild foxes from scraps placed on slates in the field. This routine continued for weeks, Joey visiting every day, appearing more and more to have developed into a wild adult fox. Then, two months after his release, we saw him for the last time. There is no certainty as to why he stopped coming back to his home, but soon afterwards a neighbour was overheard in a pub, bragging that he had shot one of Eric Ashby's foxes.

Joey, getting far too close for Fluffy the cat's comfort!

Fluffy sends a clear message to Joey, following the unwelcome invasion of her personal space

Tessa's third dog cub, Timmy, had always had a different temperament to those of Joey and Sandy. He was by far the most timid of the family (hence his name) and this wariness seemed likely to help him in the wild, keeping him away from any potential danger. Once he had left he was rarely seen. He returned to sleep in his old pen during the day only twice and, though he might have come back for food some nights, he probably found himself a territory far from home, as wild dog foxes are naturally inclined to do.

Tessa's vixen cubs at this time were still with us; the combination of vixens' natural tendency to stay with their mother and our own fear of our trigger-happy neighbours made us reluctant to release them into the wild. But the triumph of this story, and of our sanctuary, is Timmy – born and reared in captivity, of a vixen who was born and reared in captivity and now living in the wild, in his rightful and natural habitat, perhaps even fathering cubs of his own.

9 Understanding the Fox

My life has been divided more or less equally between two careers: farming and photography. There is probably no subject which sets these two professions more at odds than that of the fox. The majority of farmers are terrified at the thought of any potential predator. With their livelihoods resting with the safety of their animals, the question of how and why a predator might attack, and the true likelihood of losing any of their animals, all tend to be overshadowed by the fears themselves. Sensible, informed precautions are not even considered. More often than not, their anxiety leads them to believe that simple, reactionary destruction is the only means of protecting their stock. To the wildlife photographer, on the other hand, the fox is first and foremost a rare and beautiful animal. The settling of the highly contentious issues which surround the fox – not least that of

My first sighting of foxhounds 1930

My early photograph of a young redshank, photographed with a plate-camera in 1934

hunting – lies in the ability of country residents to understand not just one of these perceptions of the fox, but both of them. It is my interest in foxes as a photographer which has allowed me a more informed and a much more effective approach to farming. In fourteen years as a farmer, I have never lost a single animal to a fox.

In 1930, at the age of twelve, I caught my first glimpse of a fox, in the area between Fareham and Gosport in Hampshire. Soon after, I took up photography, taking snaps with a cheap plate-camera and developing the glass negatives myself before printing them in daylight on sepia paper. At the time, nature photography was considered little more than a hobby, and an unusual hobby at that. There was certainly no thought that it could ever lead to a career.

In the 1930s, farming was in decline and land was cheap. After the death of my father in 1932, there seemed little option for us other than to try our hands as farmers. In 1936, my mother, brother and I bought a cottage beside a common on the edge of the New Forest. Along with a couple of goats, we kept about eighteen laying hens which foraged on the wild common during the day and were shut up in the shed at night.

At this time, most of the residents of the New Forest owned property with common rights. These Commoners grew an acreage of oats and/or barley which they sowed by hand in the spring and cut with scythes at harvest, keeping the crop as winter feed for their livestock. Each of the small-holders also kept semi-wild ponies, a few head of cattle and several pigs, all of which were free to forage on the rough herbage. This was the first of my two spells as a resident in the New Forest, and I was privileged to witness (and to capture on film) a way of life that was about to undergo many radical long-term changes. It was also at this stage of my life that a childhood interest in the countryside developed into a lifelong passion for wildlife.

After several years of saving the tiny payments I received for sell-ing stills – even national newspapers offered as little as five shillings for each photograph they used – along with the prize money from a few competitions, I bought a cine camera and projector. Moving images added a whole new dimension to wildlife photography, a chance to represent the *behaviour* of animals. Stills enabled people to see creatures they might otherwise never get the opportunity to see; a series of stills could perhaps attempt to tell some kind of story, but the emphasis was on rarity – the camera's function was to record priv-ileged glimpses. The perspective offered by moving images meant

Hens free on the common in 1937 – on land which was owned by the residents of the New Forest

Scything oats, 1938

that these creatures could be watched over a period of time; with editing, this period could be as long as years, lifetimes, even generations. The ways of life of different, shy or rare animals could be analysed and understood by ordinary people – and the point of view no longer resembled that of an intruder but of the animal itself, as though it were the protagonist in its own story.

During my first spring exploring the New Forest, I saw what appeared to be several kittens playing in a rabbit warren amongst the gorse bushes. This was my first sighting of a litter of fox cubs. The bushes provided a perfect hiding place, and the next afternoon I managed to take four minutes' film of the cubs playing. From then on, I became obsessed with finding and filming fox earths. Most were too difficult to photograph. By and large, it was the same difficulties that apply now which prevented me then: often sites were too dark or overgrown, or sometimes too exposed; I suffered the same disappointments when the weather was too cold or wet for the animals to emerge; a change in the direction of the wind, carrying my scent towards instead of away from the subject, would mean having to abandon the chosen site for days at a time, if not altogether, perhaps most frustratingly of all, long waits at fox earths where there was no action at all for days on end would mean that I was plagued by fears that the vixen had moved her cubs elsewhere – with no way of finding out without disturbing the den, I abandoned many earths only to find out later that they had been occupied all along.

It was a whole year before I had another good opportunity. I found a den situated amongst some heather, a fair distance from a hillside. The height of the heather meant that the best viewpoint was halfway up the hill, eighty to eighty-five yards away from the earth. This was well outside the range of my few, functional camera lenses, but the position had so many advantages: as well as the certainty of a good clear view, there was at that distance virtually no risk of the vixen scenting my presence. Rather than lose this opportunity altogether, I set up a Heath Robinson affair. I removed the front from an old quarter-plate reflex camera and took the eyepiece off an old thirty-eight-inch telescope. I placed the telescope against the camera and lined the two up. That the contraption managed to focus on anything at all is perhaps something of a miracle, but the resulting series of photographs (including one of the vixen suckling her cubs) was published as a full

My first sighting of a litter of fox cubs in 1937. From then on, foxes became a passion

page in the *Illustrated Sporting and Dramatic News*, 7 October 1938, – the first time ever I had a picture of a fox published.

After three years in the New Forest, we found a suitable farm consisting of 86 acres of redland in mid Devon, an area about half a mile square with a stone and slated farmhouse and farm buildings in the centre. We kept cattle and sheep, and with the help of a couple of

My first published fox photographs taken with a Heath Robinson contraption, 1938

October 2, 1938   THE ILLUSTRATED SPORTING AND DRAMATIC NEWS   23

The "Varmint" in His Nursery Days

A New Forest Vixen and Her Litter

THESE photographs of a vixen and her cubs were taken in the New Forest between June 27th and July 5th this year, the average exposure being half a second. The vixen seldom visited her cubs during the day, and when she did, never brought any kill, although the cubs were about eight weeks old and infrequently suckled. She never remained with them more than a quarter of an hour during the time the photographer was watching. As a matter of fact, foxes eat less flesh than many people suppose, much of the damage done by poultry-killers being sheer wanton destruction. Post-mortems have proved that a favourite food of foxes is beetles.

MAMA ARRIVES: The vixen returns to her cubs. Taken at 6.15 p.m. on July 5th.

EXPECTATION: The cubs watch the return of their mother. Taken at 8.45 p.m. on June 27th.

REPOSE: Vixen and cub bask in the evening sunshine. Taken at 6.20 p.m. on July 5th.

THE EVENING MEAL: Taken at 9 p.m. on June 27th. The vixen and cubs are on a sandy clearing.

INTERRUPTION: The vixen and cub have evidently heard the photographer. A picture taken a few minutes later.

Free-range pullets on our 86 acres of redland in mid Devon

horses we grew oats, barley, mangolds, swedes, turnips and hay, which we fed to the animals. Wheat and potatoes were sold, as were eggs, poultry and surplus lambs and cattle. Ours was therefore a largely self-sufficient farm. We had up to 500 head of poultry on free range, with most of their houses out of sight of the farmhouse. In addition, I reared up to 120 geese which would wander uphill and out of sight before flying home at feeding time in one glorious gaggle. The poultry and geese were counted daily and, even during the corn harvest when the poultry houses were dragged onto the fields near the fox earths, not one bird was lost to a fox in eleven years. This was due entirely to several simple precautions, each of which seems little more than common sense to those with any understanding of the behaviour of the fox.

The most important element is the hen house. If poultry are not provided with a proper poultry house, with imitation eggs kept in tempting nests, the hens are likely to lay in cart sheds, barns or hedgerows, where they are easy prey to foxes at night. A fox, wary of the smell of man, is unlikely to take a sitting hen, but once it has the taste of poultry it becomes bold. If just one bird becomes broody and does not go to roost in the hen house, this endangers all of the other poultry. Additionally, a poultry house mounted on wheels is almost

Free-range geese had the freedom of the whole farm

impossible for a fox to get into, and an annual coating of creosote tends to deter all predators. Some of our neighbours in Devon failed to take any of these precautions and did lose poultry to foxes. (It is usually those farmers who provide their birds with the least protection, who leave them exposed and vulnerable, that are the keenest to condemn and to kill foxes.) The nearest of these neighbours was almost a mile away, and the extremely territorial nature of foxes meant that these predators were prevented from entering our farm by the presence of other foxes – foxes which had not been allowed a taste of poultry and therefore had little interest in overcoming the obstacles we had placed before them. There is a theory that there are two kinds of fox: fur and feather. Foxes learn to eat what their mothers give them. An elderly gamekeeper convinced me of this theory, explaining that if he saw cubs being fed voles, mice and rabbits, he would leave them alone. Only foxes eating birds would be destroyed. This helps explain why, with our hens safely protected, none of our geese were taken either. Fortunately, our foxes do not connect the ready-killed chicks we feed them with live hens. Tessa shows no aggression towards Happy and his pullets.

The same principles apply for sheep-farming. Simply dabbing a little *Renardine* (an animal deterrent) on the back of each new-born lamb ensured that it was safe from foxes and badgers. An even more

89

Free-range hens gleaning after the corn harvest

effective method was used by sheep-farmers in Dorset: a field was set aside and a deep, well-fenced pit dug for depositing lambing casualties and afterbirth: small wattle hurdle pens were arranged for each ewe and her new-born lambs. After a few days, when the ewe had fully recovered and the lambs had grown stronger, they were let into an adjoining field of fresh grass and the pens were used for new occupants. There was no possibility of weak young lambs being easily taken by a hungry fox. With foxes unaccustomed to eating lamb, none of these farmers' sheep was ever taken by a fox. Later on in the year, I saw a fox happily weaving its way through a flock of sheep, neither animal showing any particular interest in the other.

In these ways, an understanding approach and only a little extra trouble can make for a perfectly happy co-existence between farmers and foxes. Yet the ignorance and fear of many farmers lead them to prefer simply to destroy any potential predator – a less natural, less understanding and, above all, less efficient method of trying to protect their animals. Such action, whether shooting, snaring, poisoning or hunting, seems certain only to create more disruption and is often as damaging to farm life as to wildlife: if a dog fox is killed, his mate will become considerably more desperate to feed

Site of badger and fox earth, hidden in undergrowth

Tessa greeting Happy and his pullets without the slightest hint of aggression

their cubs, and therefore considerably more daring, perhaps finding herself forced to turn to poultry or penned gamebirds; if a vixen is killed, leaving its young, a dog fox is likely to respond with even more devastation. When the delicate balance of wildlife in the countryside is upset, the repercussions tend to be severe.

91

*

After Devon, we spent three years on a small dairy farm in Dorset (a bypass was soon proposed that eventually bisected it) before we managed to retire from farming and return to the New Forest. We moved into a small house named 'Bagber Cottage'. There was a badger sett already on the edge of the adjoining field, and it was not long before the name was changed – Badger Cottage, our present home. Without the pressure of having to run a farm, there was more time than ever before for photography. In addition to writing articles about filming wildlife, I spent 300 hours over several weeks filming badgers in the daylight. I tried to find setts which remained undisturbed all year round, as some setts are blocked by 'earthstoppers' – employed to block the setts with soil to stop a hunted fox going to ground. This upsets the badgers, and stops the cubs coming out in the early evening before dark.

I showed the films to friends, then to friends of friends. Eventually, word of my work spread to the BBC Natural History Unit at Bristol, where a producer called Christopher Parsons took a particular interest. He had been conditioning badgers in their setts to floodlights; my use of daylight and of natural evening light had resulted in scenes which looked much more natural, with regard both to the behaviour of the animals and to the lighting itself. He proposed giving up his own project immediately if I agreed to work on the programme. Still intending to remain retired, I decided to take part in this one project. Aside from Peter Scott's natural history series *Look*, there was at that time no wildlife television, nor any general level of awareness of its potential. Though I was asked to gather as much material as possible – birds, mammals, scenery, anything – I had no contract, no professional equipment, and no idea of what the BBC had in mind. All my early film, taken at the amateur speed of sixteen frames a second had to be stretched (one frame printed twice, the next one printed once, and so on) to assimilate natural movement at the television speed of twenty-five frames a second. This was expensive, time-consuming, and far from perfect, with the animals occasionally appearing to move strangely too fast. Naturally I shot future film at the professional speed. Only after two years of my amassing material in this way did a camera team come from Bristol to film an introduction for the final version: a family of visitors arrived in the New Forest and the children ran off and dreamed of spending a year there; the year consisted of my footage. The end result, *The Unknown Forest*, was a forty-five minute programme, with commentary by Johnny Morris, broadcast in 1961 when BBC1 was the only television channel and *Look* was its only regular nature programme. As television opened its own eyes to wildlife, so it helped to open the eyes of the rest of the country. At that time, few if any gift shops in Bristol sold curios or other mementoes depicting badgers, and even greetings cards showing wildlife were rare. Now the badger is perhaps the region's most enduring emblem, gracing almost anything from *objets d'art* to letterheads.

Wildlife was the Cinderella of television. The BBC's willingness to invest in nature programmes trailed slowly behind the ambitions of its Natural History Department. I was paid £400 for two transmissions of *The Unknown Forest* and £100 for fully copyright, a combined sum

Badgers in our New Forest sett

which barely covered the cost of the negatives and apparatus, let alone two years of hard work. Those involved in production, however, were kind and persuasive, and my original intention to work on only one programme was soon forgotten. I filmed several *Look* programmes, usually working on two at a time. I was expected to shoot around six to eight times as much material as would be used in the final version, enough for the editor to turn the footage into a smooth narrative. As I never used tame animals or controlled set-ups, and as I still could not afford professional equipment, each film took around two years to complete, meaning that I turned out, on average, one programme a year. I continued to work through the advent of colour television –

before colour was ever transmitted, I helped on the first ever colour nature programme, which was filmed in colour and broadcast first in black and white, then later in colour. This was probably the most exciting time to be involved in wildlife television, in at the start of something new that was blossoming into a huge and unexpected success.

I completed many episodes of *Look*, and several editions of *The World About Us*, as well as one *Wildlife on One*. Most were set in the New Forest, and they contained many shots of foxes, but *The Private Life of the Fox*, broadcast in 1975, was a film devoted entirely to my favourite animal. It was conceived as an informative study, a way of demonstrating with simple, straight-forward fact the degree to which wilfully inaccurate anti-fox propaganda had become so widely believed that many people had no idea from where they have gained such an assured image of the country fox. I filmed many hours of foxes and their cubs, enough to portray a representative study of their behaviour. My real desire, however, was to show that it was only the exceptional fox that dared to take domestic poultry.

It is difficult enough to capture on film the simple actions which make up the daily routine of wild animals. To attempt to show in one piece of footage the sort of thing a wild animal does *not* do is considerably harder. More patience than ever is necessary to film them in a position where they could do what is expected of them but choose not to. At that time, we kept a few free range hens, surrounded by three-foot high nylon netting. After many long waits, I managed to get a sequence of the fox running against the fence and the fowls fleeing in fright. Their movement scared the fox away, perhaps suggesting that it was not as daring an animal as people thought, but this was not enough. After days of waiting and waiting, the same fox re-appeared and crept under the loose netting. The hens were not frightened and the fox moved easily among them, apparently looking for any food they had left in the grass. The hens paid no attention at all to the fox's presence, and after a while the fox left the way it had entered, with barely a glance at the hens.

This scene was omitted from the final broadcast. The producer had used the first shot, of the birds fleeing, but had rejected the

Opposite – Capturing wild badgers on film in the New Forest

Right – Attracting wild fallow deer, in their dark winter coats, with calf food

second, more telling sequence. His explanation was that the material did not fit in with the popular perception of the fox. This incident epitomizes the most frustrating aspect of making films for television – the lack of editorial control. Every broadcast is inevitably an anti-climax, the reduction of years of painstaking work to less than an hour's worth of evening entertainment, with enough decent material for at least another two whole films left on the cutting-room floor.

More importantly though, this incident signifies the extent to which the general public is seeped in anti-fox propaganda. The commonly accepted image of the fox is so rarely doubted, its sources so rarely questioned, that to have shown any facts which contradicted it was, in this instance, considered simply too difficult for wildlife viewers to accept. The very service whose avowed responsibility it is to educate and inform was, in this case, too fearful of public disbelief to do anything other than perpetuate the existing untruths. The level of ignorance concerning the fox is so profound as to block the very channels through which the general public are most likely to be enlightened.

Opposite – Dog fox resting in the snow

Left – Fallow doe and fawn in spotted summer coat

One of our released foxes looking alert and ready to face life in the wild

10 The Sanctuary

By 1985, a series of mild heart attacks some years previously had forced me to give up the rather stressful business of working for television. I was continuing to take things easy, engaging in as little activity as possible, when I had my first experience of looking after a fox. Rosalind, the wife of a New Forest Verderer, had found a tiny animal in a disused pigsty. Thinking it was a kitten, she had left it alone for its mother to come and retrieve it. When she returned the next day, the animal was still there, cold and apparently dead. As she picked it up, it gave a little squeak. She took it home, phoned to ask my advice, consulted a vet, and found that she had rescued a fox cub. Six weeks

Many initially mistook Tiger for kitten, although Ginger the ca clearly wasn't fooled

later, Rosalind and the Verderer went away on holiday and we looked after the cub in their absence. Tiger – so called because of his distinctive playful growl – stayed in our living-room for a while. He was tame, but wary; he would run and hide the moment he caught sight of a camera. On their return, his owners were reluctant to re-assume the increasing responsibility of caring for the rapidly growing cub. We were delighted to keep him ourselves.

We ordered posts and wire-netting and set about making an outdoor pen. For the fencing, we used plastic-covered wire chain-link, six feet high, with an extra three feet turned in under the soil to prevent Tiger digging out, or a wild fox from digging in. At the top, I fixed an overhang of two-inch mesh chicken-netting which extended twenty inches over the fencing. As a den, I made a wooden box, two feet square and one foot high, with a loose lid and a seven-inch square entrance hole. The den was placed inside a poultry house we had stored away. After several weeks, the living-room was beginning to look the worse for wear. The pen was ready, but at this stage, Tiger had no way of knowing he was a fox. It could have been extremely damaging for him suddenly to be placed in these more natural surroundings without an older fox or a peer to reciprocate and reinforce his instincts.

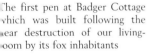

The first pen at Badger Cottage which was built following the near destruction of our living-room by its fox inhabitants

The beginnings of the sanctuary: Julian and Judy arrive from the RSPCA to keep Tiger company and to seek refuge for themselves

We managed to find an animal rescue centre in Somerset willing to give us a vixen cub to care for. After a long drive to collect it, we took the cub to the pen and released it into the run. The cub emerged very, very slowly from its container and within seconds – on spotting our cat – it gave a low call, 'wo-wo-wo'. The vixen was a dog fox. It was important to us to keep conditions as close as possible to the foxes' natural habitat, which in Tiger's case would probably have meant a litter of up to half a dozen cubs, both foxes and vixens. With this in mind, and probably with the remote possibility of our foxes one day breeding somewhere in our thoughts, we kept the new dog cub and returned to Somerset to find a vixen. This, in 1985, was how our fox sanctuary began – with Tiger, abandoned at birth, and with Julian and Judy, brought from an animal rescue centre, as much to keep Tiger company as for their own safety.

11   Tiger, Sheba and Vicky

Soon afterwards on 30 August, a young couple wrote to us from the Isle of Wight. Eighteen months earlier, they had rescued a tiny cub from a stream. It had been covered in mud and blood, but they had nursed it back to health and kept it as a pet. They named her Sheba, and she stayed with them happily as she grew into an adult vixen. They then had to move into council accommodation, where they would not be allowed to keep a fox, and so were trying to find Sheba a new home. She duly arrived at Badger Cottage on 25 September and was the tamest fox we had ever seen, welcoming everyone she saw and joyfully running towards visitors with her tail wagging in the air. Her arrival meant that we had four foxes.

Twelve days after her arrival, I noticed Sheba wandering in the field. She had managed to deform a section of the plastic-covered chain-link fencing and had squeezed through a hole little more than four inches across. I called to her and tried to persuade her to come to me. She did, but did not come close enough for me to pick her up. After a while, she made her way over to the door of her pen. To have opened the door would have allowed the other three cubs to get out and they, being younger, were less able to look after themselves and less likely to return to their own pen when they wanted to. Sheba continued to be quietly fascinated by everything around her. After half an hour or so of sniffing happily about the outside of the pens and the field, she took a determined course through our boundary fence and straight across the road – she was apparently heading

directly for the Isle of Wight, regardless of the huge distance and impossible obstacles that stood between her and the coast, let alone the Solent itself.

Sheba did not return that evening. There was still no sign of her the next morning, nor the following evening as I laid out the usual scraps on the field for the wild foxes. Then, just before dark, thirty-six hours after she left, Sheba crossed the lawn and fed greedily from the wild foxes' scraps, food which none of our kept foxes had ever touched before. When she had eaten, she came running at my call and I picked her up and took her indoors. After less than two weeks of being in the New Forest, she had come to think of Badger Cottage as her home and had returned there of her own accord. Even more impressively, she appeared to understand that it was us who fed and cared for her

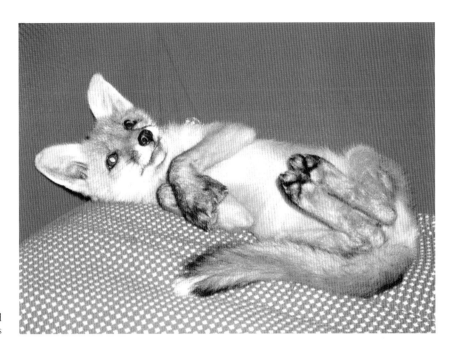

Vicky soon after we got her and recovering from mange and rickets

– she came straight to the cottage, not to the pens. It seemed wise to give the four foxes more room and so an adjoining pen was constructed with two-inch galvanized weldmesh fencing, two metres high. To prevent the foxes digging their way out, this time paths of two-feet square concrete paving slabs skirted the bottom of each fence, and the wire was held against them with pegs.

When she was a tiny cub, Vicky was found beside a road near Wimborne in Dorset, apparently having been dropped by her mother. The vixen had, perhaps, been moving her litter from one den to another, a quite common occurrence, when she was disturbed by an oncoming car. The cub was taken to the RSPCA in Bournemouth where she was reared with a litter of kittens. She was then passed to a friend of our who kept a fox, but when the two did not get on with each other particularly well, Vicky – now about eight weeks old – came to stay in our living-room. She was infected with mange mites and was suffering from rickets when she came to us. To combat the mites, every five days for five weeks we had to cover her coat in a specially medicated, frothy shampoo, before rinsing her off and

Opposite – Adult Vicky in my arms

Vicky enjoyed watching television before she left the comforts of our home for the den outside

drying her with a towel. We were at first apprehensive about having to handle her so closely, but her response was so passive that she appeared to know that the procedure was for her own benefit. Each time, throughout the five week period, her only concern was that she be allowed to play with the towel afterwards.

We kept her in the living-room for some time, introducing her to the outside world only gradually. Her first encounters with the other foxes were carried out from either side of the wire fence. Before long, she was allowed into the pens, where she developed an especially playful relationship with Sheba. Vicky was rough and demanding in her play, pulling at Sheba's ears and tail and legs. Sheba, characteristically, responded with the patience of a saint.

Tiger, our first fox, had settled in quickly and come to know us well. As with many of our later foxes, Tiger was more at ease with women than with men – perhaps like babies, all foxes seem to prefer high-pitched voices and gentler mannerisms. Tiger, in particular, would love to be stroked and petted by Eileen but tended to shy away when I went near him. By May 1986, we had had Tiger for ten months, and

he, along with Julian and Judy, the two Somerset cubs, had grown into healthy, happy adults. We decided to release all three of them into the wild. The doors to the pens were opened and, after they had gone, were left open with fresh food placed inside the pens each day. None of them was seen for two days. Then, on the third morning, Tiger appeared at our back door. He had eaten the food left for him and did not appear to be hungry, not was he injured in any way. He came to the cottage merely because he wanted to be petted and fussed over. He returned daily and, within days of his being set free, I was able as never before to pick him up and play ball with him; often he would rub his face back and forth across my hair, scent-marking me as if I were one of his own family. Throughout that summer, Tiger spent much of his time around the cottage. During the day he would hide in a hedge in the long grass, sleeping contentedly. Whenever he heard Eileen in the garden, he would re-appear, as if for a chat, but would quickly return to his chosen bed at the sound of a stranger's voice. Each evening, he would wait outside Sheba's pen. We would let him in to play with her, usually for a half-hour romp, after which we

Tiger returned frequently from the wild to be fussed over and to scent-mark us, as if to ensure that we were still part of his family

would let him out again, tired and content, to go on his way for the night. One evening, I saw him waiting as usual by the back door. Out of curiosity, I left it open for him. A few minutes later, he came shyly into the kitchen, through to the living-room, and then upstairs onto the landing, curling up where he had often slept as a cub. When I woke the next day, I found that he had not moved all night. He followed me downstairs and when I opened the door he trotted off into the morning. Tiger revelled in his new life, enjoying both the comfort which comes with captivity and the freedom of living in the wild.

One morning in September 1986, just after 6 a.m., I saw Tiger on the lawn and he seemed considerably more agitated, distraught even, altogether different from the fox that usually curled up sleepily in the sun. His demeanour was more like that of the wild foxes which visit us, constantly nervous, wariness showing in every element of his behaviour. Half an hour later, we heard hounds in the distance. The main hunting season begins in November, but from the end of August onwards the New Forest was used for 'cub-hunting', at that time an

Tiger finding scent gland on fallow buck's leg

Tiger loved to 'help' in the garden

activity which hunt associations kept very quiet. Foxes are not natural prey for hounds, so young foxhounds – the 'new entry' – have to be trained to hunt foxes. To this end, the dogs are set onto young, inexperienced cubs which are unable to look after themselves – in addition, of course, to any fully grown foxes the huntsmen come across. This out-of-season hunting, the cruellest and least sporting side of a cruel and unsporting sport, has a devastating impact. Those cubs which are captured are likely to have had little, if any, chance. Those which do manage to escape are extremely unlikely to survive, having been forced away from their family months before they would naturally have struck out on their own. Most calculatingly of all, this breaking up and dispersion of many families ensures that, by the time the main hunting season begins a few months later, there are many isolated foxes, trying to piece together a hard and unnatural subsis-

110

tence on their own. And solitary foxes, of course, are the perfect quarry for the hounds to chase and kill. This kind of cold, cruel persecution is entirely characteristic of huntsmen – yet it is somehow foxes that are thought of as 'cunning'.

We never saw Tiger again. Months later, we found out from one of the Joint Masters of the hunt that he was killed that September morning, knocked down by a hunt-supporter's car. Traffic had never been a problem for Tiger before – he had the experience and the wit to deal with crossing roads throughout the summer months when the traffic is at its heaviest. Whether his unsettled state caused his guard to slip, or whether he was deliberately run over, his death is one of many attributable to the same outdated practice – fox-hunting.

Tiger affectionately teasing a young fallow buck

Opposite – Jack and Jill were cubs brought to us by the RSPCA after they were unearthed by a bulldozer

12   Jack and Jill

After Tiger's disappearance, Sheba ate nothing for four days. We then began to get some idea not only of the sense of community that exists between foxes, but also of their loyalty. The death of any fox is felt severely by the foxes around it. Sheba mourned for months, completely losing all interest in visitors, and we despaired of ever seeing her happy again.

The following spring, on 21 May 1987, the manager of the local RSPCA asked us if we would be willing to take in two cubs which had been unearthed by a bulldozer. He specifically requested that they be reared with a view to their being set free as soon as possible. We insisted that their eventual freedom should be left to our own discretion and we invited him to inspect the conditions in which our foxes were kept. When he saw the size of the grass runs and the arrangement of the pens, he suggested that we keep the cubs as long as we wanted, saying simply that they would be better off with us than in the wild. The two cubs were a dog and a vixen of about five weeks old, each unusually hesitant and wary, perhaps understandably so. We named them Jack and Jill, and to begin with kept them downstairs in the box-room. After a few days, we introduced them to Sheba. They were allowed into her pen only for a short while each day. From the moment of their first meeting, Sheba became a different vixen. She took to the cubs as if they were her own, rolling over onto her back in delight and thrusting her legs in the air. The cubs accepted her just as easily, apparently thrilled to

have found a new mother. That was the first of many times that Sheba would demonstrate her maternal instincts. For years afterwards, her happiness was helped by the care and attention she lavished on each new injured and abandoned cub that was brought to us.

When introduced to Jack and Jill, Sheba was delighted with the young cubs and soon recovered from her grief for Tiger

Jack grew up to be a beautiful fox

Jack and Jill

By the following spring, Jack and Jill had grown into strong, healthy foxes. The pair were still more wary than those of our cubs that had been with us from an earlier age, and though Jacky had tamed considerably over the year, Jill had become a permanently cautious vixen and seemed very likely to survive in the wild. We released her in May, leaving food in her pen until it was no longer taken. We saw little of her from then on, until, after six months of her having returned to the wild, I noticed that the grass had been scraped away from the wire of her old pen. Later that morning, I saw her at the lower end of the field, where she was obviously in trouble. She was having tremendous difficulty walking; her back legs seemed to be paralysed. We left the door of her old pen open and placed some food in her old house. That night, we found her lying flat out in her sleeping-box. Our first instinct was to take her to a vet, but the traumatic effect of moving her while she was in so vulnerable and agitated a state seemed likely to do as much harm as good. Instead, we left her injuries to heal themselves and gave her the food, the care, the attention and the time for her to recuperate. Within three weeks, she had recovered sufficiently to go on her way again.

When Jilly returned to us at her old home she showed great trust

We continued to see Jill from time to time in the months that followed. During the winter, she and a wild mate made themselves a den in the natural badger sett in the corner of our field. By spring, she had given birth to a litter of cubs. They were only a few weeks old, too young to have emerged from their earth, when we heard a dog yapping relentlessly at the sett. By the time we saw what was happening, there was a fox-terrier barking excitedly with its head and body down the hole, and there was nothing we could do. The next morning, I found the remains of a headless cub next to Jilly's old pen. She must have carried the body there all the way from her earth to the safety of her old home. There were no other remains, and no more live cubs.

Jilly struggled on and continued to survive. She still came to the cottage occasionally, feeding from scraps or taking a little food from our hands. The following year, she made her home in some rabbit holes, not far from her old den, but this time actually in the forest, where she was less exposed to the sort of danger that had recently cost her so much. She produced another litter, this time of five cubs, and she would often bring them from their earth to eat the food left on our lawn. Around the cottage, she acknowledged us and treated us much as she had always done; but away from our property, she was as wary as a wild fox. I managed to take only one picture of her in the forest before the click of the camera caused her to flee. A year later, having spent three of her four years living in the wild, Jilly died of kidney failure. She had been looking poorly for some time, and our suspicions were aroused when we saw her drinking frequently. She returned to spend her last days in the artificial badger sett, painfully but peacefully ending a short life – but one that was much longer than average for a country fox. Eventually, it seemed, the difficult weeks of her infancy, combined with the stress of twice producing (and once losing) her young, took their toll. Perhaps most importantly, her second litter of cubs had been successfully weaned, and were now old enough to fend for themselves.

Opposite – Jilly at her den in the New Forest where she was as wary as a wild fox

A year before her death, Jill's brother Jacky, became the father of Tessa. In February 1994, sadly, Sheba died. She was ten years old and had become increasingly sleepy, snoring contentedly in her den for much of the day. One morning, I found her lying in the sun, weak and unable to stand. Later, when the sun had moved on and she was in shadow, I carried her gently into her favourite house, where she drifted peacefully away. Sheba was a truly wonderful fox, who made a lasting impression on all who were privileged to meet her. We miss our gentle Sheba terribly and will never forget her.

Foxhound running by the fox pens

13 New Forest Fox Sanctuary Today

The deterioration of the foxes' habitat here has accelerated considerably in recent times. The effect on those foxes who have been with us for some years is unmistakable. Tessa, in particular, is a completely different fox from the happy young vixen cub who welcomed so many visitors in her first year. There is one cause: fox-hunting.

The New Forest is over hunted. At the other extreme, Ashdown Forest is the site for only two hunts each year. Elsewhere the average fox-hunt meets two or three times a week during the season and have a much larger hunting area than the New Forest. In fact the New Forest had a total of 165 meets of the three hunts – fox, fallow buck and hare. Fortunately things have changed since 1997 when the New Forest Buckhounds gave up fallow deer hunting which considerably reduced the number of meets we had to endure by one third. The hunts are licensed by the Forestry Commission to operate only on Crown land and are expected to keep their hounds away from certain restricted areas such as the Bolderwood Deer Sanctuary, Queen's Meadow and other sensitive land. The hunts are not allowed on the ten acres of our private property around Badger Cottage, where, until recently, it was legal for hounds to approach our land and hunt right to our boundaries. Consequently hounds have strayed, chasing foxes which had gone to ground in the badger sett at the edge of our field.

For years we had asked for a restriction on hunting too close to our land. Now at last the new Government has agreed to a no-go area at

least a hundred yards beyond our boundary. If only this could have been arranged years ago; it would have saved so much stress for our foxes – and ourselves. The badger sett would also have been left in peace and would now be fully occupied.

We now feel much more optimistic for the future of our local wildlife. Eventually we trust that all hunting with dogs will be banned by government policy.

Unfortunately, the Forestry Commission can still order that all badger setts in the vicinity of the scheduled meets be blocked on hunting days. Their argument is that this prevents foxes from going to ground and the hounds from digging at and damaging the setts. The underlying truth is that the hunts' refusal to train the hounds not to dig at earths and setts is tacitly acknowledged and accepted. In all of the three years of my first stay in the New Forest, I found only one badger sett blocked and only one other destroyed by the hunts' terrier men digging out and killing a fox that had gone to ground. Then, setts were interfered with, on average, about once a year; now, during the hunting season, they are blocked around three times a month. Huntsmen can no longer be bothered to train their hounds properly. Badger setts are blocked at every meeting, and they are never unblocked.

A badger family in the New Forest

Badgers are sensitive animals, and this relentless disturbance certainly prevents them from breeding and probably shortens their lives. The badger population in the New Forest has declined as rapidly as the standards of the huntsmen. In the 1960s, there were around twenty badgers in the natural and artificial setts in our field. Now there are one or two individuals, and there have been no cubs for five or six years. The badgers deserted the setts altogether on 29 January 1991, just when Tessa was shortly to give birth to her litter. In the middle of the day, hunt riders were heard galloping on the road. Half an hour later, hounds arrived in the woodland alongside our land, the fox they were chasing probably having gone to ground in one of the badger setts. There was a cacophony of whip-cracking, galloping horses, shouting and yelling, horn-blowing and baying hounds, all just a few yards from our foxes' pens. All of our foxes, including the pregnant Tessa, began to run around in their pens, anxious and distraught. They never hide in their houses at these times: their fear seems to paralyse them, and their inability to hide in the most obvious place could be simply because they are too scared; but it is more likely that the instinct not to lead the hounds straight to their dens and their

121

families is no less powerful in captivity. A complaint to the Joint Master met with this response: 'They'll soon get over it.' Another time he said, 'Can't you put them in your bathroom on hunting days?'

The hunt returned twice on 19 February and 2 March. On the last occasion, the hounds were even more out of control. Six of them ran to the recently deserted badger sett; another went straight to the fox pens and stood on its hind legs to look in. Hours later, Vicky was still crouching behind a door, too frightened to move. It was four hours before she lifted her head. Our foxes are sensitive animals even at their most relaxed. They understand precisely the significance of the baying hounds and the blasting horns that surround them and their fear is horrendous. As the years have passed and the public disapproval of fox-hunting has increased, so the huntsmen have become more defensive, more belligerent, less mindful of the effect they have on the environment. We are waiting to see what the effect of the new severe restrictions on the hunt will be and how they will affect us. The attitude of the hunting fraternity has hardened, and the impact is obvious, not least in the behaviour of our foxes. They still react to us in a friendly, trusting manner; but where once they had eagerly and delightfully welcomed visitors, now they run and hide at the slightest sound of a stranger.

Opposite – Cautious baby Johnny, with Tessa, keeping an eye out for danger

Foxhounds on our badger sett

Gentle Tessa with me – still as trusting as ever with both of us

We have now decided not to take on any more foxes owing to advancing years. I am eighty-one and inevitably less active. It would not be fair to any new arrivals should we cease to be able to care for them properly. Consequently we thought it best to set free a dog fox and vixen, along with their eight-month-old cubs, providing them with back-up food in their runs for as long as they needed. It appears to have worked well for all but for the one dog, Johnny, who returned to his old home badly injured after a fortnight of freedom. His genitals had been badly torn and bitten. Perhaps he had been challenged by another fox, dog or even a badger. However, the problem was how to give him antibiotics when he was refusing all food and would surely spit out any bitter-tasting pill. Fortunately the solution was simple – crush the antibiotic pill to a powder, add a little sugar, mix with butter or margarine, then spread on the upperside of a front paw. This worked like a charm for Johnny immediately licked off the mixture without hesitation throughout the full course of treatment. Following

New Forest Fox Sanctuary Today

Following some unfortunate experiences in the wild, Johnny secured a happy future as Tessa's companion at the sanctuary

the antibiotics he has recovered well, but as his serious injury will prevent him ever having cubs and we feel that he is unable to look after himself in the wild, he will provide a perfect companion for Tessa. They now sleep very happily together and have become inseparable.

I had rescued Johnny in 1997, when he was about four weeks old. He was very weak and lay limp in my hands, so I brought him home and syringed a little Lactol into his mouth as he was obviously unable to take solid food. His hindlegs were lifeless which was a big worry. After several days on Lactol, he was able to enjoy a little tinned cat-food. From that moment on, his strength gradually returned and his delight at being able to become active again was wonderful to see. Immediately the appropriate name of 'Johnny Walker' flashed into our minds.

Suzie still comes at night for food left under a carton outside the back door. If we see her she comes to a call and takes a chick from our fingers and we are able to see how well she looks. As she comes after midnight we wonder if her den is some distance away. Gradually the freed foxes will disperse as they find their own natural sustenance and territories. One or two young vixens may have cubs nearby, which happened when Suzie set herself free and no doubt we will be helping with their needs in due course.

Suzie still comes to the back door for food – left for her under a carton – usually after midnight or early in the morning as this picture shows

Tessa and Johnny are safe in our sanctuary but we will be anxious on hunting days. It is the uninformed acceptance of the portrayal of the fox as vermin which allows the barbaric sport of fox-hunting to exist at all. Meanwhile we hope that this book has gone some way to changing that acceptance, and to portraying the fox as it really is – a rare and beautiful animal no more deserving of cruelty than any other.

A forest stream in autumn. Chief Seattle would have approved of this environment

Fallow deer in our wild daffodils. Chief Seattle loved the animals and the natural scene

We know the white man does not understand our ways. One portion of land is the same to him as the next, for he is a stranger who comes in the night and takes from the land whatever he needs . . . .

His appetite will devour the earth and leave behind only a desert. I do not know. Our ways are different from your ways . . . .

I have seen a thousand rotting buffaloes on the prairie, left by the white man who shot them from a passing train. I am a savage and I do not understand how the smoking iron horse can be more important than the buffalo, that we kill only to stay alive . . . .

What is man without the beasts – If all the beasts were gone, man would die from a great loneliness of spirit. For whatever happens to the beasts, soon happens to man. All things are connected. Whatever befalls the earth, befalls the sons of the earth. If men spit upon the ground, they spit upon themselves. This we know: the earth does not belong to man: man belongs to the earth. This we know. All things are connected like the blood which unites one family. All things are connected. Man did not weave the web of life: he is merely a strand in it. Whatever he does to the web he does to himself.

From Chief Seattle's letter to the President
of the United States, 1854